Sounds of the Sun

A book of poems

Clyde McCulley

CONTENTS:

Sound of the Sun

the sound of the sun

the sound of the sun

lying in bed

he hears the sun rise

forest full of trees

trees full of birds

birds full of song

he rises, feels for his cane

shuffles his way outside

to the warmth of the sun

and orchestra of birds

turns towards the rays

that he cannot see

opens his ear lids and

smiles at the morning

wind

Sound of the Sun

wind

wind gently bends blade

of grass into a graceful arc

can uproot a large tree

with an unexpected wind burst

waves over the clover

making little paths

for fairies to run

creates musical notes

as it forcefully rounds the

corner of an old sea captain's

house on the bay

make music as lips

blow over the mouth hole

of a flute

slowly pumps water

as it turns an old

farm windmill

powers wind turbines

on the desert of California

spins a pinwheel held in

hand of a small child

blows a gentle breeze

across a boy's body as he lies

in the shade of an old apple

tree in the heat of summer

a force that one can

hear, feel, use, observe

the results of

but never see

14

15

the hummingbird and o'keefe

the hummingbird and o'keefe

a hummingbird soars

with swift speed to

a large planting of

bee balm flowers

suddenly stops in mid air

hovers, backs up, flits

right and left stabbing its

long beak into the opening

of one flower after another

in and out, in and out, its

little tongue thrusting into

each like it was an intimate

georgia o'keefe flower painting

summer nights

summer nights

curtains hang lifeless

awaiting breeze that does not come

whippoorwill sings

it's hot and sweaty song

it doesn't feel like singing

boy hears whistle's blast

of a night train

slowly crawling its way

through the country side

breaking the silence at each crossing

ambulance sirens scream

through hot night air

transporting wounded

following its own wail

down highway to hospital

bird's song fades

as does whistle and siren

air is impotent

boy falls asleep

soaked in sweat

smells of wind

smells of wind

wind blows over plowed
fields

brings smell of approaching rain

      farm boy marvels at the power of smell

city child plays in rain on streets

wind blows smell of rot and piss

      he dislikes the power of smell

mother smells approaching rain

hastens to gather clothes from the line

      thankful for the power of smell

26

symphony on a tin roof

28

symphony on a tin roof

boy hears sounds of gathering storm

thunder shatters silence

bolt lights the room

rain drops hammer out its

tin roof symphony

awake listening watching

counting 1001, 1002, 1003

guessing distance to lighting's strike

hears vicious crack of

bolt's attack

daylight illumines large oak, split

struck for the third time

tree is cursed, daddy says

boy thinks squirrel should

find a different home

a gull or an angel

a gull or an angel

watching a gull
catch an up current of air

higher and higher
until it was so small
I could not see it

maybe it was an
angel returning home

or a gull who was
seeking freedom

wonder if gull knows

kris kristofferson's line

"freedoms just another

word for nothing left to lose"

or knows jonathan livingston seagul

who loved to fly

was a loner and visionary

who had to find himself

he learned love and

returned to the flock

that expelled him

to share his new gained wisdom

but was it freedom?

shame and lies

36

shame and lies

when summer was over

we had to put on shoes

and go back to school

I dreaded this time of year

the first day the teacher

would ask the students

to recite where they had

gone on vacation during summer

I was ready

I had sent for publicity

on various vacation spots

when it was my time I told

stories about going

to Washington DC

Niagara Falls and

other wonderful places.

then at Christmas, she would

ask what presents we got from Santa

some got bikes and dolls and more

again I would lie

why did she not understand

that several of us were poor

and a little short on money

FDR helped the poor

with some things

but he did not send some of us a Santa

kite and boy

42

kite and boy

inexpensive paper kite

flutters in the wind

making wonderful sounds

back to the boy holding

the other end of the string

kite dips and smiles

at boy and dances

little jigs as its string

is held taut

boy smiles back

a strong wind begins to blow

kite string breaks with a snap

startled boy looks up

at the kite as it starts to

fly erratic patterns and

crashes to earth

boy runs across field

tears run down

his face

afraid what he will find

as he nears he sees

the kite trying to lift itself

from the ground

it stops trying but manages

to give the boy a smile

t

he boy and the kite

will fly again tomorrow

when its broken stick is repaired.

the sun will beam and

the kite and boy will smile

47

a room with a view

a room with a view

a room with a view

can be numerous things

a view down a country lane

a view down a garbage filled alley

a view from a cabin in the woods

a view from a prison cell

a view from a high-rise apartment

a view from a basement apartment

a view from a lover's room

a view from an orphanage

a view of earth from a spacecraft

a view from a hospital room

a view from a cottage on the sea

a view from a widow's room to the cemetery on the
hill

a view from the rear window

(hey what is that guy bagging up

in the apartment across the way)

reminiscing

52

reminiscing

when one is poor

it doesn't take much

to make one happy

happiness does not

come from money

it comes from experiencing

small things in life

he remembers mama's

biscuits and gravy

fried okra and

homemade cakes and pies

winter evenings

the family gathering

around the radio

imaging each story heard

sitting on metal lawn chairs

in the deep dark of summer

watching fireflies dashing

illuminating the landscape

simply talking in the

tranquility of the night

listening with interest

to the other's thoughts

he crawls into bed

smiling about today

eager about tomorrow

sleep comes slowly

Sound of the Sun

About the author

Clyde McCulley is a retired college professor of art. He has published several books and is now writing poems, many relating to his own childhood. This is his first book of poetry.
He lives in Portland Maine with his wife Susan and cat Shadow.

Books published by the author

The Boy on Shady Grove Road

The Boy after Shady Grove Road

Panther Creek Mountain: The Big Adventure

Panther Creek Mountain: The Haunted Pond

Panther Creek Mountain: Twin Tree house Mystery

Journals

Six word stories

I fondly remember my Grandparents

Childhood Memories

All are available on Amazon Books

Sound of the Sun

Sound of the Sun

.